Contents

GH00790204

4

①

STRAWBERRY AND BANANA SMOOTHIE

100g strawberries
1 small ripe banana
1½ tsp honey
200ml ice
150ml coconut milk or dairy milk
Garnish: 1 fresh strawberry

Place strawberries, banana, honey, ice and milk in the 800ml beaker and use the stick blender on high for 15 to 30 seconds, until mixture is smooth.

Pour into a glass. Slice the strawberry (not cutting right through) and slot on the side of the glass.

②

HONEY CHOCOLATE PEANUT BUTTER

120ml whole milk
25ml peanut butter
25ml honey
10ml cocoa powder
30ml protein powder
(chocolate or vanilla whey)
½ banana
200ml ice

Place milk, peanut butter, honey, protein power, banana, cocoa powder and ice in the beaker provided.

Use the blender to pulse, and then on high for 15 to 30 seconds.

5

MIXED BERRY PROTEIN

50g blueberries
50g strawberries
50g peaches
50g mango
30ml protein powder
(chocolate or vanilla whey)
300ml orange juice
200ml ice

Place blueberries, strawberries, peaches, mango, protein power, orange juice and ice in the 800ml beaker.

Use the stick blender to pulse, and then on high for 15 to 30 seconds.

CHEF TONY'S CITRUS PUNCH SMOOTHIE

2 oranges (peeled and sectioned)
75ml powdered milk
3 tbsp powdered sugar
3 drops orange extract
½ tsp vanilla extract
170ml cold water
240ml ice

Place all ingredients (except ice) in the beaker provided.

Using the blender, mix on high until chopped. Add half the ice and blend for 1 minute.

Add remaining ice and blend until smooth and frothy!

6

PIÑA COLADA

120ml coconut milk
120ml pineapple juice
60ml rum
25g white sugar
140ml ice

In the beaker provided, mix the coconut milk, pineapple juice, rum, sugar and ice.

Take the blender and pulse to mix ingredients, and then blend until smooth.

Garnish with a slice of pineapple on the rim of the glass.

Add a scoop of ice cream to make the Piña Colada really creamy

STRAWBERRY DAIQUIRI

200ml ice
25g white sugar
30g frozen strawberries
7ml lime juice
30ml lemon juice
45ml rum
15ml lemon-lime flavoured carbonated drink

Place ice, sugar, strawberries, lime juice, lemon juice, rum and lemon-lime drink in the 800ml beaker.

Take the stick blender and pulse to mix, then blend until smooth. Garnish with whipped cream and a strawberry.

3

MARGARITA

450ml tequila
225ml triple sec
4 tbsp sugar
225ml fresh lime juice
800ml ice
2 tbsp salt
6 lime wedges

Combine tequila, triple sec, lime juice,
2 tablespoons of sugar and ice in the
800ml beaker.

Take the stick blender and use on low to mix,
then high for 15 to 30 seconds to smooth.

Mix salt and remaining sugar in a shallow bowl.
Moisten rim of glass with lime wedge and dip
rim into the sugar and salt mixture.

Pour margarita into glass and garnish with lime.

4

MUD SLIDE

60ml vodka
60ml coffee liqueur
60ml Irish cream
180ml vanilla ice cream
60ml chocolate syrup

Place vodka, coffee liqueur, Irish cream, ice
cream and 30ml chocolate syrup in the
800ml beaker.

Using the blender, start on low and then pulse
and increase speed until mixture is smooth.

Take the remaining 30ml chocolate syrup and
swirl into the mixture. Pour in a glass to serve.

Top with whipped cream for a real treat!

Perfect for use in stir-fries or as an accompaniment to Chinese dim sum

This dressing works particularly well as a marinade for lamb or chicken

8

GINGER

150ml soy sauce
75ml rice wine vinegar
35ml corn oil
1 tsp sesame oil
1 tbsp toasted sesame seeds
2 spring onions (whites only)
2 cloves garlic
1 tbsp honey
2 tbsp crushed fresh ginger
1 tsp tomato paste

Place all ingredients in the beaker provided.

Using the stick blender, mix on high for 30 seconds. Taste and add a little more sesame oil if required.

Pour into glass jar and refrigerate for 1 hour.

CREAMY BUTTERMILK

300ml low-fat buttermilk
100g mayonnaise
50g fresh coriander
1 medium ripe avocado
1 clove garlic
1 large shallot
1 lime (juiced)
1/8 tsp cumin
1 tsp celery salt
Fresh green pepper, halved and seeded (optional)

Place all ingredients in the 800ml beaker.

Using the whisk attachment, whisk on low until all ingredients are mixed.

Add salt and pepper to taste.

This dressing works particularly well with fish dishes

CHEF TONY'S CITRUS

150ml extra virgin olive oil
lemon (juiced)
1 tsp white vinegar
tsp fresh oregano
tsp garlic powder
tsp onion powder
Salt and pepper (to taste)

Add all ingredients (except the oil) to the 800ml beaker.

Using the whisk attachment, mix together. Slowly add a steady stream of olive oil and whisk on low until all ingredients are fully mixed.

Add salt and pepper to taste.

CHEF TONY'S SICILIAN

150ml balsamic vinegar
150ml extra virgin olive oil
1 garlic clove
1 tbsp honey
1 tsp ground mustard
1 tsp dried chives
tsp dried oregano
1 tbsp grated Romano cheese
Salt and pepper (to taste)

Place all ingredients (except the oil) in the 800ml beaker.

Using the whisk attachment, mix until the sugar is dissolved. Slowly add a steady stream of olive oil and whisk on low, until all ingredients are mixed.

Add salt and pepper to taste and serve on a bed of fresh green leaves.

10

SPINACH AND ARTICHOKE BAKE

250g cream cheese
400g artichoke hearts, drained
(using chopper processor)
800g frozen spinach (thawed and
chopped – in two batches)
100g mayonnaise
100g Parmesan cheese
100g Romano cheese
1 clove of minced garlic
(using chopper processor)
1 tbsp fresh basil
½ tsp salt
½ tsp black pepper

Preheat oven to 180°C/365°F/Gas 4

Place cream cheese, mayonnaise, Parmesan cheese, Romano cheese, garlic and basil in the 800ml beaker.

Using mini chopper processor, pulse, and then mix well. Turn out into a large bowl, add the chopped artichokes and spinach and mix well.

Place in baking dish in the oven for 25 minutes or until the top is brown.

Serve with toasted bread or as a side dish.

11

12

CHEF TONY'S ANTIPASTO DIP

400g artichoke hearts (drained)
150g quark (low fat cheese)
6 slices pepperoni
10 pitted Kalamata olives
65g shredded mozzarella
85g canned mushrooms
90g marinated roasted red peppers
1 stalk celery
1 tsp onion powder/granules
1 clove of garlic
2 tbsp Italian seasoning
1 tsp of lemon juice
Salt (to taste)

Mix all ingredients in the mini chopper processor until smooth and serve with breadsticks or tortilla crisps.

Great topping for chicken or swordfish

MEDITERRANEAN SPICES AND OIL

100ml olive oil
1 tsp dried basil
1 tsp dried thyme
½ tsp dried rosemary
½ tsp dried Italian seasoning
1 clove fresh garlic
50ml sun-dried tomatoes (from jar)
1 tbsp grated Parmesan cheese
1 tsp tomato paste
Salt (to taste)
Red chili pepper flakes to taste
(optional)

Add ingredients to 800ml beaker and use the Chef Tony handheld food processor on high until smooth.

Serve with toasted bread.

Marinate chicken in the seasoning overnight; also great as topping for fish

14

MANGO DIP

1 mango, peeled
1 avocado, peeled, pitted, and diced
400g canned tomatoes, drained
1 green chili, seeded and minced
25g chopped fresh coriander
1-2 cloves garlic, minced
1 tsp salt
30ml fresh lime juice
40g chopped red onion
45ml olive oil

In the 800ml beaker combine the mango, avocado, tomatoes, jalapeno, coriander and garlic.

Stir in the salt, lime juice, red onion, and olive oil. Use the stick blender to chop and blend the flavours.

Refrigerate for about 30 minutes before serving. Serve with tortilla chips.

15

This is an excellent topping for swordfish

SALSA

2 medium plum tomatoes
¼ red chili (seeded)
½ onion
2 tbsp coriander leaves
1 tbsp olive oil
Pinch of salt
Lime juice (to taste)
Garlic (optional)
Freshly ground pepper (to taste)
Juice of one lime
Little garlic (to taste)

Add ingredients to 800ml beaker and mix with the stick blender.

Pulse to mix ingredients and blend until salsa is to desired texture.

Serve with tortilla chips.

16

Salsa is a great healthy topping to add to chicken or fish

17

18

SALMON BRUSCHETTA

190g salmon fillets or 100g of
smoked salmon
(depending on taste preference)
95g cream cheese, softened
50g sour cream
8 spring onions, finely chopped
1g salt
¼ tsp hot pepper sauce
2 tsp fresh lemon juice
1 tsp Worcestershire sauce

In a medium saucepan of simmering water, poach the salmon fillets for 10 minutes, or until flaky and tender.

In the mini chopper processor, mix together cream cheese, sour cream, green onions, salt, hot pepper sauce, lemon juice and Worcestershire sauce. Flake salmon into the mixture.

Cover and refrigerate for 8 hours, or overnight, before serving.

Serve with toasted bread.

19

20

BEAN DIP

400g can of cannellini beans,
drained and rinsed
2 garlic cloves
Juice and zest of a whole lemon
2 tbsp thick Greek yogurt
1 tsp cumin
¼ tsp cayenne pepper
1 tbsp fresh parsley
Salt and pepper (to taste)

Place ingredients in the mini chopper processor.

Pulse to mix, then blend to achieve the desired texture.

Serve with toasted pita chips or tortilla chips.

21

CHEF TONY'S SMASHING AUBERGINE DIP

1 large aubergine, halved
1 beef tomato, hulled and sliced into quarters
60ml mascarpone cream
1 spring onion
2 tbsp olive oil
1 tsp Italian seasoning
½ tsp onion powder
1 tsp garlic puree
Salt and black pepper (to taste)

Heat oven to 200C/400F/Gas 6.

Place the aubergine on a baking sheet with parchment paper split side down.

Drizzle with olive oil. Bake for 30 to 35 minutes.

Scoop out aubergine from skin and place all ingredients into chopper processor and blend.

Serve with French bread, sliced and brushed with olive oil and garlic and toasted in the oven until golden.

23

24

CHEF TONY'S COLESLAW

½ small green cabbage
½ small red cabbage
1 large Korean pear, cored and peeled
(optional if not in season)
1 large carrot
100g raisins
150ml mayonnaise
3 tbsp apple cider vinegar
1 tbsp honey
¼ tsp ground turmeric
2 tbsp chopped fresh coriander
Salt and pepper (to taste)

Remove the stem portion of the cabbage and cut into small wedges.

In the multi-function processor with slicing blade, process both the red and green cabbage.

Change blades to the shredding blades and shred the Korean apple and carrots.

Remove top and add all remaining ingredients. Mix together and taste.

Adjust spices to suit your taste and enjoy!

25

HOUMOUS

400g canned chick peas (drained)
100ml tahini (sesame paste)
3 tbsp extra virgin olive oil
1 cloves garlic
1 large lemon freshly juiced
(or 4 tbsp of lemon juice)
¼ tsp smoked paprika
½ tsp ground cumin
½ tsp of salt
½ tsp of white pepper
Chili pepper flakes (optional)

Combine ingredients in a suitable bowl and mix with the stick blender until smooth.

Serve with baked or toasted pitta or carrot batons.

SPICY YUMMY YOGHURT DIP

150ml thick Greek yogurt
1 medium green chili (seeded)
½ tsp coriander
1 tsp lemon juice
1 clove garlic
Salt and white pepper (to taste)

Place all ingredients in the 800ml beaker.

Using the blender, mix until smooth.

Serve with crisps or breadsticks.

This is great served alongside my houmous

CREAMY CORN AND VEGETABLE

28

100g canned sweet corn
100g diced tomatoes
250ml vegetable stock
250ml chicken stock
½ small onion, cubed
1 stalks celery, cubed
1 small carrot, cubed
1 small courgette
250ml full fat milk
Salt and pepper (to taste)

Place all ingredients into a stock pot and bring to a boil, stirring occasionally.

Turn down heat and simmer for 20 minutes. Use the stick blender on high until fully mixed and thickened.

Serve with herby croutons.

29

CHEDDAR ALE

4 thick-cut bacon slices, cut into 3-inch strips
2 tbsp unsalted butter
1 large yellow onion, diced
2 carrots, peeled and diced
2 celery stalks, diced
3 garlic cloves, minced
70g plain flour
300ml pale ale
1 tbsp Worcestershire sauce
600ml full fat milk
600ml chicken broth
550g sharp cheddar cheese, shredded with chopper
Salt and freshly ground pepper (to taste)
Toasted croutons (garnish)
Olive oil (for drizzling)

In a stock pot or large saucepan, cook the bacon until crisp. Allow bacon to cool and drain.

Add one tablespoon of the fat into the pot, reduce the heat to medium and melt the butter. Add the onion, carrots and celery, cover and cook, stirring occasionally, until the vegetables are softened (about 20 minutes).

Add the garlic and cook for 1 minute. Add the flour and cook, stirring occasionally, for 3 to 4 minutes. Add the ale and cook, stirring constantly, for 2 to 3 minutes.

Add the Worcestershire sauce, milk and broth, increase the heat to medium-high and bring to a simmer. Reduce the heat to medium-low and simmer for 10 to 12 minutes.

Remove the pot from the heat and use the stick blender to puree the soup until smooth.

Set the pot over medium-low heat and add the cheese by the handful, stirring constantly; do not allow the soup to boil. Season with salt and pepper.

Ladle the soup into warmed bowls and serve immediately.

Garnish: Use croutons and the bacon and drizzle with olive oil.

31

BUTTERNUT & SWEET POTATO SOUP

1 large butternut squash
(1.5 – 1.8kilos)
1 large sweet potato
150g unsalted butter
2 yellow onions, chopped
8 fresh sage leaves, shredded or
1tsp dried oregano
1.1L chicken or vegetable stock
(this can be made from stock cubes)
Salt and freshly ground pepper
(to taste)
Ground nutmeg (to taste, if needed)
Pinch of sugar (if needed)

32

Preheat an oven to 200°C/400°F/Gas 6.

Prick each squash with the tip of a knife (to stop it exploding when it bakes). Place the whole squashes on a baking sheet and roast (for about 1 hour) until they feel soft to the touch and a knife penetrates the skin easily.

Remove from the oven and, when cool enough to handle, cut in half lengthwise and remove and discard the seeds and fibres. Scoop out the pulp into a bowl and set aside.

In a saucepan over low heat, melt the butter. Add the onions and half of the sage and cook, stirring occasionally, until the onions are tender and translucent (8 to 10 minutes).

Add the stock and squash pulp, raise the heat to high and bring to a boil. Reduce the heat to low and simmer for a few minutes to combine the flavours. Remove from the heat.

Use the stick blender on high and pulse, and then hold to the bottom of the pot to puree the soup.

Reheat gently over medium-low heat. Season with salt and pepper. If the squash is starchy rather than sweet, a little nutmeg will help. If the nutmeg does not give the proper flavour balance, add a pinch of sugar.

Garnish: Use the remaining sage and add a dash of double cream when blending to make a smoother, richer soup.

Roasting the squash makes it easier to peel and seed, and deepens the flavour of its flesh, producing a richer, more flavourful soup

33

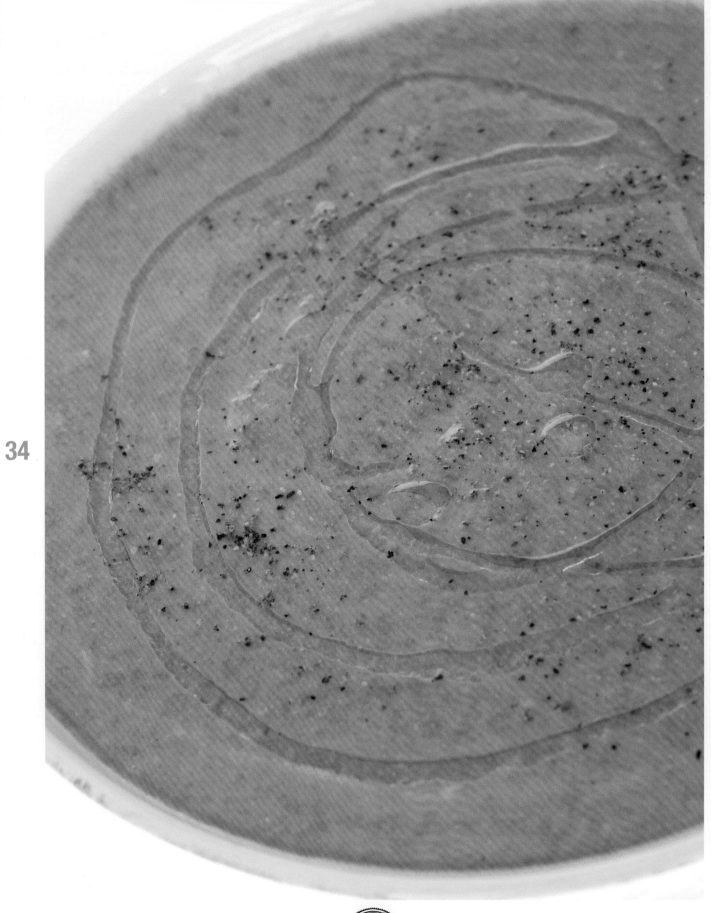

34

CREAMY SPINACH

240g frozen chopped spinach
(thawed and drained well)
550ml chicken stock
(from stock cubes or fresh)
150ml full fat milk
50g instant mashed potato
½ tsp crushed garlic
½ tsp crushed ginger
15g butter
50g Gruyère cheese
Salt and pepper (to taste)

Add all ingredients (excluding potato) to a saucepan and bring to a boil.

Reduce heat and simmer for 10 to 15 minutes.

Add potato flakes and use the blender to thicken and smooth.

35

CREAMY TOMATO

800g can whole Roma tomatoes
400ml vegetable stock
(broth may be substituted)
2 tbsp tomato paste
2 cloves roasted garlic
1 tsp sugar
2 tsp olive oil
400ml double cream
1 large white potato
(cubed and boiled)
1 tsp each of salt and pepper
Fresh basil (to garnish)

36

Place all the ingredients into a stockpot and bring to a boil.

Simmer for 20 minutes.

Take the stick blender and pulse and blend until smooth.

37

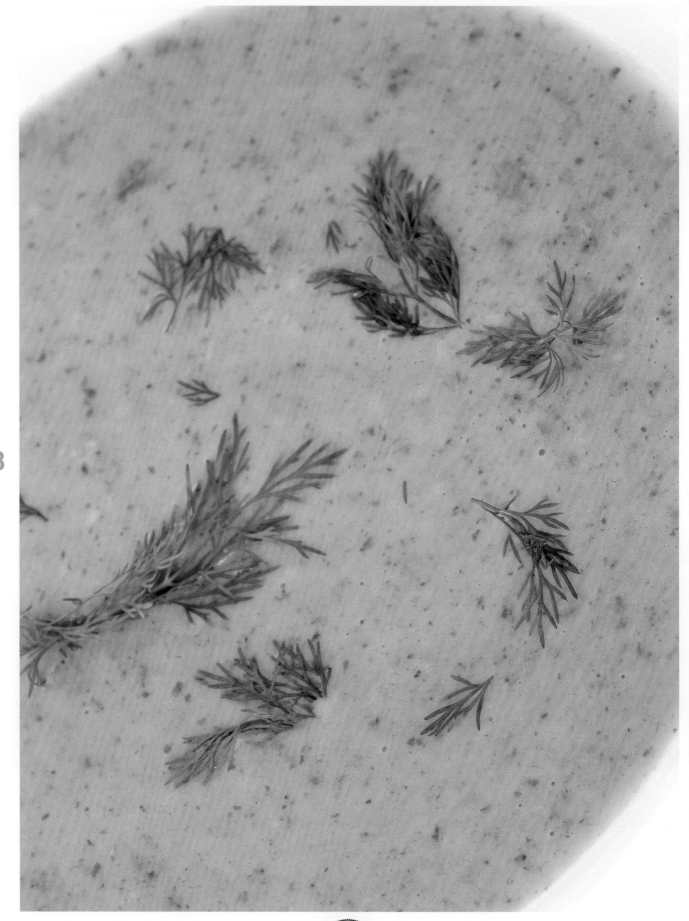

VICHYSSOISE - POTATO AND LEEK

3 tbsp olive oil
2 leeks, including tender green portion, rinsed and coarsely chopped
2 fennel bulbs, thinly sliced (reserve leaves for garnish)
2 baking potatoes, peeled and coarsely chopped
1.8L chicken or vegetable stock (or prepared broth)
1 bunch watercress, stems removed
½ cup double cream
Salt and freshly ground white pepper (to taste)

In a soup pot over medium heat, warm the olive oil.

Add the leeks and sauté, stirring occasionally, until soft (4 to 5 minutes).

Add the fennel and potatoes and sauté, stirring occasionally, until slightly softened (about 10 minutes).

Add the stock and bring to a simmer. Cover partially and cook until the vegetables are completely softened (about 20 minutes).

Add the watercress and cook until it is wilted, but is still bright green (about 2 minutes). Remove from the heat.

With the stick blender, puree the soup in stock pot until smooth. Stir in the cream and season with salt and white pepper.

Refrigerate for at least 4 hours. Ladle the soup into chilled bowls.

Garnish: Use the left over fennel leaves for garnish.

39

Select creamy-coloured fennel bulbs with no browning, topped by crisp stems and feathery green leaves. Cut the stems off about 2 inches from the bulb and use only the bulb, trimming away the base of the core if it is thick and tough. The leaves can be used for flavouring soups and salads

CURRY

2 tbsp peanut oil
1 tbsp margarine
1 large onion (chopped)
1 tbsp minced fresh ginger root
2 tbsp minced garlic
1 tsp ground cinnamon
1 tsp ground black pepper
2 tbsp ground coriander
2 tbsp ground cumin
¼ tsp ground turmeric
1 tsp cayenne pepper
2 tomatoes
2 green chilies (seeded)
100g fresh coriander
150ml full fat Greek yogurt, whisked
until smooth
3 cups water

40

Heat oil and margarine in a small skillet or wok over medium-high heat.

Add onion and sauté until very brown (10 to 15 minutes). Add ginger and garlic to onion and sauté for an additional 2 minutes. Process mixture in the multi-function food processor until smooth. Do not rinse processor.

Place onion mixture in a large saucepan. Stir in the cinnamon, black pepper, coriander, cumin, turmeric and cayenne pepper and cook over low heat until mixture is thick and has the consistency of a paste.

Puree tomatoes, chili peppers and coriander in food processor until smooth. Add to onion mixture and stir well over low heat, cooking off moisture from tomatoes and coriander.

Add yogurt a little at a time, stirring constantly to avoid curdling. Blend the whole mixture in the multi-function food processor to puree or use the stick blender in the saucepan.

Return to saucepan, add water and increase heat to high to bring sauce to a boil. Cover saucepan and boil for 3 to 5 minutes.

Reduce heat and simmer until desired consistency is reached.

To serve with meat: cook the meat first separately, and then simmer for 5 to 10 minutes in the sauce before serving over rice or with bread. To serve with vegetables: steam raw veggies first for 4 to 5 minutes, then simmer for 5 to 10 minutes in the sauce before serving

TARTAR

Juice of 1 lemon
2 whole eggs
350ml rapeseed
1-2 chopped dill pickles
1 shallot, finely chopped
2-3 tbsp chopped fresh chives
1 tbsp chopped capers
Salt and freshly ground pepper (to taste)

Add the lemon juice and egg yolks to the beaker provided. Place the stick blender in the beaker and process in short pulses until smooth.

With the motor running, add the oil in a slow, steady stream and process until smooth and blended.

Transfer to another bowl and fold in the pickles, shallot, chives and capers. Season with salt and pepper. Refrigerate until ready to use.

CHEF TONY'S CRAZY PEPPERCORN SAUCE

600ml beef stock (using cubes if needed)
3 tbsp brandy
100g crème fraiche
2 shallots
2 tbsp dehydrated mushrooms
2 tbsp dehydrated onions
1 garlic clove
1 tbsp cornstarch
1 tbsp dry mustard powder
1 tsp of black peppercorns

Place all ingredients (excluding the crème fraiche and cornstarch) in a stock pot and bring to a boil.

Reduce heat and simmer, to reduce the mixture by 50%. Add the crème fraiche and cornstarch to the 800ml beaker and mix slowly using the whisk attachment.

Add the mixture slowly into the reduction in the stock pot and whisk until smooth.

42

4

REMOULADE

150ml Chef Tony Mayonnaise or any
bought mayonnaise
5 sprigs fresh parsley
1 small sweet pickle
½ tsp garlic powder
1 tsp English mustard
1 tsp lemon juice
3 dashes Worcestershire sauce
1 tbsp dried chives or alternatively half a
shallot
Salt and pepper to taste)

Place ingredients in the beaker and use the
whisk attachment to combine. Serve chilled.

*This is excellent as a dipping sauce for
chicken, steak, seafood and even veg*

5

CHEF TONY'S
HOME-MADE KETCHUP

28oz whole tomatoes in puree
1 small onion
2 tbsp olive oil
1 tbsp tomato paste
1 cup brown sugar (packed)
150ml rice wine vinegar
¼ tsp salt
¼ tsp white pepper

Place all ingredients in a pot, and gradually
bring to a boil, stirring occasionally.

Turn down heat and simmer for 20 minutes.

Use the hand blender to blend until smooth.

MARINARA

28oz can of whole Roma
tomatoes in juice
28oz can of tomato sauce
3 cloves of garlic
½ onion
3 tsp Italian seasoning
1 tsp sugar
4 tsp olive oil
¼ cup fresh basil
Salt and pepper (to taste)

Place olive oil, garlic and onion into
beaker and mince ingredients.

Pour into stock pot and cook for 2 to 3
minutes until onions are translucent.

6

43

Add all other ingredients (excluding
basil). Bring to a boil, lower heat and
simmer for 45 minutes, stirring frequently
to avoid burning.

Use stick blender on high until smooth,
taste and adjust seasonings to liking.

Take basil and chop in chopper
processor on low until coarsely chopped.

Add to the sauce, let it stand for 5
minutes and serve.

Serve with pasta and add shaved
Parmesan or Romano cheese.

Add fresh basil at the end; adding this at the beginning would result in a bitter taste, as it would be overcooked

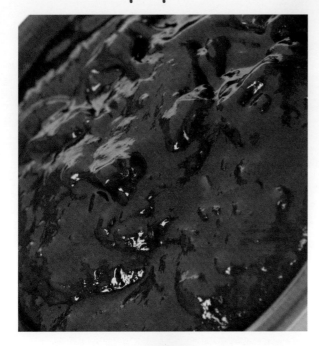

44

SWEET KICKIN' BBQ MAGIC

400ml Chef Tony's Ketchup
(or any bought ketchup)
½ small onion
2 large garlic cloves
100ml apple cider
100ml apple cider vinegar
100ml water
3 tbsp brown sugar
1 tsp cocoa
½ tsp instant coffee
1 tbsp black treacle
2 tbsp mustard powder
2 tbsp honey
1 green chili (seeded)
120ml Worcestershire sauce

Place all ingredients into a pot and bring to a
boil, stirring occasionally.

Turn down heat and simmer for 20 minutes.
Blend using the stick blender until smooth.

BOLOGNESE

600ml Chef Tony's Marinara Sauce
450g lean beef mince (or turkey mince)

Add Chef Tony's Marinara Sauce to your
chosen mince.

Serve with pasta and add shaved Parmesan
or Romano cheese.

BÉARNAISE

150ml white wine
150ml white wine vinegar
1 large shallot (peeled)
1 tsp tarragon
215g unsalted butter
3 large egg yolks
½ tsp salt
Dash of white pepper (to taste)

Add ingredients to a bowl and place over saucepan of simmering water.

Use the whisk attachment and mix until smooth.

BEST BLUE CHEESE EVER

225g blue cheese
225g cream cheese
2 chopped shallots
75ml milk or cream

Add ingredients to the mini chopper processor and mix.

Add cream cheese and blue cheese, then pour in milk and mix until smooth.

Garnish with shallots.

PAN SEARED JERKY JUMBO SHRIMP

16 jumbo shrimp
(peeled and de-veined)
2 eggs
100g plain flour
100g cornmeal
2 tbsp unsalted butter
3 tbsp olive oil
2 tbsp Old Bay spice
2 tbsp jerk spice
1 tsp garlic powder
Dash of salt and pepper

Beat eggs in a bowl.

In a large plastic bag, add flour, cornmeal and all spices. Seal and shake bag until all ingredients are mixed.

Place shrimps in bag, seal and shake. Remove shrimps and add to eggs. Place shrimps back into the bag, shake and coat a second time.

Place oil and butter into a large skillet and melt over medium-high heat. Place shrimps into a hot pan and brown (about 3 minutes each side).

Remove from pan and set aside for 3-5 minutes. Serve with Chef Tony's tartar sauce, a side of green vegetables and mashed potatoes.

47

48

CHEF TONY'S OUTDOOR INDOOR RIBS

2 racks of pork ribs
Salt and pepper
Garlic powder
Chef Tony's Sweet Kickin' BBQ Magic

Preheat oven to 170°C/325°F/Gas 3.

Wash and dry ribs. Sprinkle both sides of ribs with salt, pepper and garlic powder.

Place on a non-stick baking pan. Cover with aluminum foil and bake for 3 hours.

Remove ribs, uncover and pour off excess water and grease. With a brush, baste both sides with Chef Tony's Sweet Kickin' BBQ Magic.

Turn up heat in oven to 450°C/230°F/Gas 8 and bake, uncovered, for 30 minutes.

Baste both sides again with a generous amount of the BBQ sauce and bake for another 20 minutes.

Turn oven to grill, baste ribs with more sauce and cook until crispy brown on both sides.

Remove and leave to stand for 10 minutes.

49

Serve with corn on the cob, fresh beans and
extra sauce to dip into!

NONNA'S BAKED PASTA

900g pasta (any variety)
450g pork mince
450g beef mince
1 large onion (chopped)
Dried oregano
150g grated Parmigiano-Reggiano cheese
300g shredded mozzarella
1 litre Béchamel sauce

Bring 6½ litres of salted water to the boil.

Add pasta and cook for 8 minutes or until almost cooked, but a little firm in the centre (al dente). Drain well and set aside.

In a large, non-stick skillet add pork and beef and cook until slightly brown. Drain off excess fat and set aside.

In a large baking dish, place 150ml of Béchamel sauce; enough to cover the bottom of the dish.

Add one third of the pasta, followed by one third of the meat, grated cheese and mozzarella, then top with 300ml Béchamel sauce.

Repeat step 5 twice with remaining ingredients. Top with remaining Béchamel sauce, cover and bake in a preheated 190 degree oven for 1 hour.

Uncover and turn oven to grill Sprinkle with a little more Parmigiano-Reggiano cheese and grill until top is golden brown.

52

STEAK KABOBS

900g sirloin steak
(cut into 1" cubes)
150ml olive oil
1 tsp onion powder
3 tbsp Herbes de Provence
3 large garlic cloves
6 large wooden skewers
150ml béarnaise sauce

Add olive oil, garlic, onion powder and Herbes de Provence into beaker.

Using stick blender, blend on high for 30 seconds. Place beef cubes into large bowl, pour on herb mix, toss and refrigerate for 1 to 2 hours.

In a rectangular dish, add cold water and soak skewers for 1 hour.

Preheat BBQ*. Place 5-6 cubes on each skewer, then place on the BBQ and cook for 3 minutes per side (for medium rare).

Remove from BBQ and allow to rest for 10 minutes.

Top each skewer with béarnaise sauce, with a side of almond string beans and wild rice.

*Can be cooked in a preheated oven at 220°C.

53

SALMON FRITTERS

54

1 can (440g approx) pink salmon
3 eggs, separated
3 tbsp flour
½ tsp salt
Dash of pepper
½ tsp garlic powder
1 tbsp minced parsley

Remove skin and bones from salmon and mash.

Beat egg yolks until light and thickened, using the whisk attachment.

Beat in flour, salt, pepper, garlic powder, parsley, and salmon.

In another bowl, beat egg whites until stiff. Fold egg whites into first mixture.

Using a tablespoon, drop portions of mixture into hot, deep fat.

Fry salmon fritters until nicely browned.

56

BAKED CHICKEN IN PEPPERCORN SAUCE

6 x 170g fresh chicken breasts
Cling film
200g plain flour
2 eggs
3 tbsp extra virgin olive oil
Smoked paprika
Salt and pepper

Preheat oven to 190°C/375°F/Gas 5.

Rinse and dry chicken breasts. Cut each from top to bottom, but not all the way through. Open and set aside.

Place large piece of cling film on cutting board and place chicken breast in the centre. Cover with another piece of cling film. Using a mallet, pound from centre of breast to the outside, evenly flattening each breast.

Place flour in a bowl with paprika, salt and pepper and mix well.

Add eggs and oil into another bowl and beat well with the whisk attachment.

Dip chicken breast into flour, then into egg and back into flour, coating each one evenly.

Place on non-stick baking pan and gently fry for 35 minutes.

Let it rest for 10 minutes. Serve each breast topped with peppercorn sauce with sautéed carrots and spinach.

57

POTATO CROQUETS

900g white potatoes
(quartered and cooked)
110ml rapeseed oil
3 eggs
165ml milk
55g mashed potato flakes
110g Italian seasoned breadcrumbs
110g shredded mozzarella cheese
55g grated Parmigianino-Reggiano
55g parsley flakes
Salt and pepper (to taste)

Add all ingredients (except the eggs and breadcrumbs) into the large food processor with chopping blades.

Mix for 2 minutes on medium speed. Taste and adjust seasoning to your liking.

Beat the eggs, then add to mixture and blend on high for another minute or so until a smooth consistency is achieved.

Using a large spoon, make equal sized scoops onto a waxed paper-lined baking dish.

Place a scoop of potato mix into your hands and form into a thick sausage shape (about 7.5cm long).

Place in breadcrumbs and roll until evenly coated. Repeat until all your potato mix is rolled and coated.

Add oil to a large skillet and heat on high for 1 to 2 minutes. Place 3-4 croquettes into frying pan and cook on each side until golden brown.

Remove and drain on paper-lined platter.

This is a typical side dish served with meats and fish. I use the leftovers for breakfast with eggs and ham!

59

KIM'S CHICKEN BURGERS

400g diced chicken
1 tsp chopped fresh tarragon or dill
60g rough chopped red onion
50g chorizo
Salt and black pepper

Put all the ingredients in the mini chopper and process.

Shape into burgers and gently fry or grill until cooked through (5 to 10 mins).

SMASHED CAULIFLOWER

900g frozen cauliflower
60ml shredded Cheddar cheese
60ml shredded Parmesan cheese
500ml chicken broth
30ml butter or margarine

Bring chicken broth to a boil. Add frozen cauliflower and boil for about 8 to 10 minutes.

Drain and add cheeses, butter and more broth if it is too thin for your taste.

Using the stick blender, mash in the saucepan until you get the consistency of mashed potatoes.

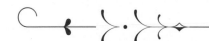 

SICILIAN FIG COOKIES

500g plain flour
1½ tbsp baking powder
¼ tsp salt
110g sugar
150g vegetable shortening
1 large egg
1 tbsp vanilla
150ml full fat milk
400g dried figs, soaked in water
About 14 Medjool dates with stones removed
250g raisins
150ml honey
1 tsp cinnamon
150g orange marmalade
85g walnuts or almonds, coarsely chopped
1 large egg white beaten with 1 tbsp water for egg wash
Coloured sprinkles

Sift the flour, baking powder, and salt into a large bowl. Add the sugar and stir well. Cut in the shortening with a fork and work the mixture through.

In a bowl, use the stick blender on low to mix the egg, vanilla, and milk together. Add to the flour mixture and work the mixture with your hands into a rough dough.

Turn the dough out onto a floured work surface and knead for 5 minutes, or until smooth. The dough will be soft. Cut the dough into 4 pieces, wrap each piece in cling film and chill for 45 minutes in the fridge.

To make the filling: grind the figs, dates, and raisins in the food processor until coarse (this ideally should be done in two batches). Place the mixture in a bowl, add the honey, cinnamon, marmalade and nuts and mix well. The mixture will be thick. Set aside.

Preheat the oven to 190°c. Lightly grease 2 baking sheets. Divide the dough into quarters and work with 1 piece of dough at a time, keeping the remaining dough covered.

On a floured surface, roll out each piece of dough to a 12-inch square. Cut the dough into 4 rectangles (about 7cm long), and place a tablespoon of the filling mixture down the centre of each rectangle.

Carefully fold over the long edges of each rectangle to meet in the centre, and then pinch the seam to close it securely. Turn the cookie seam side down.

Pinch the ends to close and fold them under. Shape the cookies into crescents and place seam side down on the cookie sheets.

Make 2 or 3 diagonal slits in the top of each crescent with scissors. Brush with the egg wash and sprinkle with coloured sprinkles.

Bake for 25 minutes, or until golden brown. Transfer to wire racks to cool.

64

CAPPUCCINO CHEESECAKE

150g dark chocolate covered
digestives biscuits
60g unsalted butter (melted)
500g mascarpone cheese
125ml crème fraiche
3 tbsp instant coffee granules,
dissolved in 3 tbsp just-boiled water
125g caster sugar, plus 1½ tbsp
(for the topping)
4 whole eggs, plus 1 egg yolk
240ml sour cream
cocoa powder, to dust

Put the biscuits in chopper and process until they become crumbs, then combine with the melted butter.

Tip the mixture into a greased tin, 20cm. Smooth out and press down to make an even base. Cover and chill in the fridge for at least 30 mins.

Preheat the oven to 180°C/350°F/Gas 4. Use stick blender on low setting to mix the mascarpone and crème fraiche until smooth, and then stir in the coffee and sugar. Beat in the eggs until well crumbled.

Pour the mascarpone mixture over the base. Put in a roasting tin and pour water around the cake tin so that it reaches one-half to two-thirds of the way up the sides.

Bake in the pre-heated oven for about 50 minutes, until set, but soft. Stir the remaining 1½ tablespoons of sugar into the sour cream.

Remove the cheesecake from the oven, gently spoon over the sour cream, spreading it out evenly, and then return to the hot oven for 10 minutes.

Remove from the oven, let it cool and then cover and chill for at least 4 hours or overnight. When ready to serve, carefully remove from the cake tin and dust with cocoa powder.

65

PANETTONE BREAD PUDDING

50g butter, softened (optional)
250g panettone, about 5 medium
slices (If unavailable use brioche)
2 eggs
142ml carton double cream
225ml milk
1 tsp vanilla extract
2 tbsp caster sugar
Icing sugar (for sprinkling)
Softly whipped cream (to serve)

66

Preheat the oven to 160°C/325°F/Gas 3 and grease a 850ml pint shallow baking dish with a little butter.

Cut the panettone into wedges, leaving the crusts on. Butter the slices lightly. Cut the slices in half and arrange them in the dish, buttered side up.

In a bowl, use the stick blender to whisk together the eggs, cream, milk, vanilla extract and sugar and pour evenly over the panettone.

Put the dish in a roasting tin and pour hot water around it to a depth of about 2.5cm. Bake for 35 minutes until the pudding is just set - it should be yellow inside and nicely browned on top.

Dust with icing sugar and serve with whipped cream.

67

LEMON MERINGUE

200g white sugar
2 tbsp plain flour
3 tbsp cornstarch
¼ teaspoon salt
450ml water
2 lemons, juiced and zested
2 tbsp butter
4 egg yolks, beaten
1 (9 inch) pie crust, baked
4 egg whites
6 tablespoons white sugar

Preheat oven to 175°C/325°F/Gas 3.

To make lemon filling:
In a medium saucepan, whisk together 1 cup sugar, flour, cornstarch, and salt. Stir in water, lemon juice and lemon zest and cook over medium-high heat, stirring frequently, until mixture comes to a boil. Stir in butter.

Place egg yolks in a small bowl and gradually whisk in half a cup of hot sugar mixture.

Whisk egg yolk mixture back into remaining sugar mixture and bring to a boil; continue to cook, while stirring constantly, until thick.

Remove from heat and pour filling into baked pastry shell.

To make meringue:
In a large glass or metal bowl, whip egg whites until foamy. Add sugar gradually, and continue to whip until stiff peaks form.

Spread meringue over pie, sealing the edges at the crust. Bake in preheated oven for 10 minutes, or until meringue is golden brown.

69

CHOCOLATE PECAN BROWN TART

375g Chef Tony's pastry
125g salted butter
100g plain chocolate, chopped
200g golden caster sugar
2 eggs
1 tbsp vanilla extract
4 tbsp plain flour
125g pecan halves, roughly chopped
Crème fraîche to serve

70

Heat oven to 200°C/400°F/Gas 6. Roll out the pastry and use to line a 24cm tart tin. Chill for 15 minutes in the freezer or 30 minutes in the fridge.

Line with baking paper and baking beans and bake for 10 minutes. Take out the beans and paper and bake for another 5 minutes.

Allow to sit while you make the filling. Turn oven down to 180°C/365°F/Gas 4.

Melt the butter and chocolate in a large glass or metal bowl, set over a pan of boiling water.
Note: ensure the water does not touch the bowl.

Use the stick blender to mix in the sugar, eggs and vanilla, then the flour.

Stir in the pecans, pour into the tart case and bake for 30 minutes.

Cool then serve with crème fraîche.

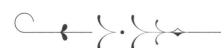
CUSTARD TART

300ml of full fat milk
3 tbsp cornstarch
½ vanilla pod
100g white sugar
6 egg yolks
500g shortcrust/puff pastry

Preheat oven to 190°C/375°F/Gas 5.

Lightly grease 12 muffin cups and line bottom and sides with puff pastry.

In a saucepan, combine milk, cornstarch, sugar and vanilla. Cook, stirring constantly, until mixture thickens.
Place egg yolks in a medium bowl.

Slowly whisk half a cup of hot milk mixture into egg yolks. Gradually add egg yolk mixture back to remaining milk mixture, whisking constantly with whisk attachment.

Cook, stirring constantly, for 5 minutes, or until thickened. Remove vanilla pod.

Fill pastry-lined muffin cups with mixture and bake in preheated oven for 20 minutes, or until crust is golden brown and filling is lightly browned on top.

73

74

SICILIAN ORANGE SORBET

300ml orange juice
2 star anise
100g caster sugar

Boil the orange, star anise and sugar together until the sugar has dissolved.

Remove the star anise and allow to cool.

Put mixture into a freezer-proof container, removing every few hours to whisk with stick blender. This will help break up the ice crystals and provide a perfect sorbet.